PATHWAYS TO PROSPERITY

UNLOCKING MULTIPLE REVENUE STREAMS TO FINANCIAL INDEPENDENCE

MICHAEL SCHULZ

SCHULZ PUBLISHING

Legal Notice

Disclaimer Notice

CONTENTS

10. References   57

EPILOGUE

"The MOST effective way of bringing in passive income is educating people."

– Jess Van Den

I personally feel that the #1 benefit of having my expenses covered by passive income is that I get to keep doing a lot more of the kind of work I enjoy. I also get to work the way I want to work – where I want, when I want, how I want, and with whom I want."

– Steve Pavlina

"If you're still doing what mommy and daddy said for you to do (go to school, get a JOB, and save money), then you're losing."

– Robert Kiyosaki

INTRODUCTION TO YOUR FINANCIAL FREEDOM JOURNEY

Welcome to the exciting world of financial freedom! Imagine waking up every morning knowing your money works for you, not the other way around. This book is your key to unlocking that reality.

Money flows in many streams. Think of a river with its twists and turns, branching off into smaller creeks and tributaries. Your financial life can be just as rich and varied. You no longer need to rely on a single source of income. The days of putting all your eggs in one basket are over. You hold in your hands a roadmap to financial diversity. Each page reveals secrets to creating multiple income streams. These aren't just ideas – they're proven strategies successful people use worldwide. People like you who dared to dream bigger.

Financial independence isn't just for the wealthy elite. It's for anyone willing to learn and take action. This book breaks down complex concepts into simple, actionable steps. You'll discover how to:

- Start a business that aligns with your passions.

- Invest wisely in stocks, real estate, and more.

- Generate passive income while you sleep.

- Leverage your skills into profitable side hustles.

But this journey is about more than just making money. It's about creating a life of freedom and purpose. When you have multiple income streams, you gain control over your time and choices. Imagine being able to pursue your dreams without worrying about a paycheck. That's the power of financial diversification. As you read, picture yourself building a solid financial foundation. See yourself confidently navigating economic ups and downs. Feel the peace of mind from knowing you're prepared for whatever life throws your way.

This book isn't just about theory—it's a call to action. Each chapter ends with practical steps you can take right away. Small actions compound over time, creating significant results. Your journey to financial freedom starts now, with the turn of each page. Are you ready to transform your financial future, break free from the limitations of a single income, and create a life of abundance and opportunity? Then, let's begin. Your path to prosperity awaits.

The Importance of Financial Diversification

Picture your financial life as a garden. A garden with only one type of plant is fragile. A single storm or pest could wipe it out. But a garden bursting with different plants? That's a garden that thrives no matter what. Financial diversification is the key to a thriving money garden. It's about planting many seeds of income. Some will grow tall and strong, and others might struggle. But together, they create a lush landscape of financial security.

Why does this matter so much? Let's dive deeper.

The world we live in is changing fast. Jobs that were once secure are now uncertain. Think about relying on just one job for all your money. What happens if that job disappears? What would you do? Suddenly, your entire financial world crumbles. It's like balancing on one leg—any slight push can knock you over. This is a risk many people face when they rely on just one source of income.

But when you have multiple income streams, you stand firm. If one source dries up, the others keep flowing. You're no longer at the mercy of a single employer or market whim. This is the essence of financial diversification—spreading risks and giving yourself security. Diversification is about more than just protection. It's about growth. Different income streams can feed each other. Money from one source can help grow another. It's like cross-pollination in your financial garden.

Imagine the freedom this brings—no more living paycheck to paycheck. No more having more month than money and no more sleepless nights worrying about job security. Instead, you have options. You have breathing room. You have the power to shape your financial future. This isn't just for the rich and famous. Anyone can start diversifying their income. It might begin small—a side hustle here, a small investment there. But like seeds in fertile soil, these small starts can grow into mighty oaks of financial strength, providing a financial safety net.

Diversification also opens your eyes to new opportunities. You start seeing potential income everywhere. That hobby? It could become a profitable side business. That empty room? It could generate rental income. Your knowledge? It could turn into an online course that earns while you sleep. Remember, financial diversification is a journey, not a destination. It's about constantly exploring, learning, and adapting. You're not just making money as you grow your various income streams. You're building resilience. You're creating freedom. You're shaping a future where financial worries fade away, replaced by a sense of security and endless possibility.

Are you ready to start planting your diverse financial garden? The seeds of your prosperous future are waiting. Let's get growing.

Overview of Multiple Revenue Streams

Money flows in many forms. Picture a river branching into smaller streams, each bringing life to different parts of a landscape. That's how multiple revenue streams work in your financial world. What are these streams? There are various ways to bring money into your life. Some flow fast and strong, like a rapid. Others trickle steadily, like a gentle brook. Together, they create a powerful current of financial stability. These streams could include a regular job, running a small business, investing, or even earning from hobbies.

Let's explore these streams:

Active Income: This is the most familiar and usually the starting point for most people. It's the money you earn by trading your time and effort and includes your salary, wages, tips, and any other compensation you receive for your labor. Your job, freelance work, or running a business falls here. It's direct and often flows quickly. However, relying solely on active income can be risky. If you lose your job or can't work, your income stops.

Passive Income: Imagine earning money while you sleep. That's passive income. Rental properties, royalties from books or music, or earnings from a well-established online business fit here. Once set up, these streams can flow with minimal effort from you.

Portfolio Income: This is money your money makes for you. Dividends from stocks, interest from bonds, or profits from selling investments at higher prices than you paid. It's like planting money seeds and watching them grow. However, it often requires a good understanding of financial markets and a willingness to take on some risk.

Why are multiple streams so powerful? They provide security and opportunity. If one stream slows down, others can pick up the slack. You're not relying on a single source for all your financial needs.

Multiple revenue streams can come from various activities or investments. For example, you might have a full-time job that pays your bills, but you also write a blog that generates advertising revenue. Maybe you've invested in the stock market or own rental properties. Or perhaps you create and sell handmade crafts online. Each of these activities generates income and contributes to your financial portfolio.

Think about a musician. They might earn from live performances (active income), royalties from recorded music (passive income), and investments in other artists (portfolio income). Each stream supports the others, creating a symphony of financial stability. Or consider a teacher who writes educational books. Their salary is active income, and book royalties become passive income. Investing some profits in the stock market adds portfolio income. Each stream reinforces the others, building a more robust financial foundation.

These streams aren't just for the wealthy or famous. Anyone can start building them. A small side business, a rental property, or learning to invest can be your first steps. As you learn and grow, so do your streams. The significant part is that you don't need to stick to one thing. Mix and match different income sources to find what works best for you.

Multiple revenue streams also bring freedom. They give you options. Want to take time off to travel? Your passive income might cover expenses. Looking to change careers? Other income streams can support you during the transition. Remember, building multiple streams takes time and effort. It's like learning to play an instrument. At first, it might feel awkward. But with practice, you create beautiful music—or, in this case, a harmonious financial life.

Are you ready to explore these streams? To dip your toes in new financial waters? The adventure of building your river of wealth awaits. Let's discover the potential flowing all around you.

The Goal of Financial Independence

Dream with me for a moment. Picture a life where money worries fade away, where you wake up each day free to choose how you spend your time. This is financial independence. It's not just a dream—it's a goal you can achieve.

Financial independence means your money works for you. You're no longer chained to a paycheck. Your investments, businesses, and passive income streams all come together to support your lifestyle. It's like having a money machine that runs on its own. This doesn't mean you stop working altogether; rather, you have enough income from various sources to support your lifestyle without depending solely on a paycheck.

But why is this goal so powerful?

Freedom! That's the heart of it. Freedom to pursue your passions without worrying about bills; freedom to spend time with family and friends; freedom to travel, learn, grow, and give back to your community. Financial independence opens doors you might never have imagined.

Imagine saying goodbye to the daily grind. No more rushing to beat the morning traffic and no more working long hours for someone else's dreams. Instead, your time becomes genuinely yours. Want to start a charity? Go for it. Fancy learning a new language or instrument? You've got the time. Your days become filled with purpose and joy, not just earning a living.

Financial independence also brings peace of mind. Economic ups and downs? They don't keep you up at night. Job market changes? They don't threaten your security. You've built a fortress of diverse income streams that can weather any storm. This goal isn't about becoming ultra-wealthy. It's about having enough—enough to live comfortably, enough to pursue your dreams, enough to help others. It's about quality of life, not just quantity in your bank account.

Clear goals can help you stay focused and motivated. What do you want to achieve with your money? Are you saving for a new home, retirement, or your children's education? Maybe you want to travel the world or have enough to live comfortably without financial stress. Imagine taking a vacation whenever you want or buying something you need without worrying about the cost. Understanding your goals will help you choose the right income streams and strategies.

How do you reach this goal? It starts with a shift in thinking. Stop seeing money as something you trade time for. Start seeing it as a tool for creating more opportunities. Each dollar becomes a seed you can plant and grow.

Building multiple income streams is vital. Your job might be one stream. Investments could be another. A side business, rental property, or created content that keeps earning—all add to the flow. Assessing your skills and interests is crucial. What are you good at? What do you enjoy doing? These questions will help you identify potential income streams that bring money, joy, and satisfaction while matching your strengths and passions. As these streams grow, they replace your need for traditional work.

To help you achieve this, the book is divided into chapters that will guide you through identifying, creating, and managing multiple income streams. We'll look at different types of income, such as active, passive, and portfolio incomes. Each type has its advantages, and we'll explore what might work best for your situation. Keep in mind that the journey to financial diversification is personal and unique to each individual. There's no one-size-fits-all approach, but anyone can develop a robust financial portfolio with the correct information and some creativity.

Remember, financial independence is a journey. It doesn't happen overnight, but each step you take brings you closer. Each new skill you learn, each investment you make, and each income stream you create builds momentum. Are you ready to start this journey? To break free from financial worries and enter a life of true freedom? The path to financial independence lies before you. It's time to take that first step. Let's walk this path together toward a future where you control your time, choices, and destiny.

THE POWER OF FINANCIAL DIVERSIFICATION

I n this chapter, we'll explore the concept of multiple revenue streams. We'll examine what they are, why they're beneficial, and what types you can incorporate into your financial strategy. By diversifying your income sources, you can enhance financial security and take steps toward financial independence.

Definition and Benefits

Financial diversification through multiple income streams may be a new or foreign concept to you. Although the idea of having multiple revenue streams has been found throughout history, financial diversification is relatively new and not taught in traditional education. So, let's take a moment to examine what multiple revenue streams are, their benefits, and their importance.

What Are Multiple Revenue Streams?

Multiple revenue streams mean earning money from more than one source. Instead of relying solely on a regular paycheck from a job, you could have other sources of income like a side business, the money you make from a hobby, rental properties, or earnings from investments.

Having multiple streams means you have various ways to earn money, making your financial situation more secure. It's like having many faucets of income, not just one. Some flow fast, others trickle, but together, they create a strong financial river. This approach helps increase your income and protects you financially if one source fails.

Advantages of Diversified Income

The primary benefit of having multiple revenue streams is financial resilience. If you lose your job, for example, you'll have other income sources to help you manage your expenses without panic—losing one source doesn't mean losing everything. Whether it's an unexpected expense or a downturn in the economy, diversified income gives you a cushion to fall back on.

Additionally, with extra sources of income, you can make more money overall. Even if each stream only brings in a little bit, they can add up to a lot. This can help you achieve your financial goals quicker, whether those goals include saving for a big purchase, eliminating debt, or investing more into your retirement fund. Diversified income sources can also lead to a more fulfilling work life. You might find passion in a side hustle that isn't just about making money but also about enjoying what you do. This can reduce work-related stress and increase overall job satisfaction. Imagine doing what you enjoy most in the manner you want and on your schedule.

Another significant benefit is flexibility. With multiple income streams, you might have more control over your time. Some income sources don't require you to work a typical nine-to-five job. This could allow you to choose when and where you work, which is great if you want to spend more time with your family or travel. Best of all, you can become your own boss and skip all the bureaucracy and policies that make having a job irritating and unfulfilling. But, most importantly, that side hustle or business can become the reason that drives you to have a positive social impact and have a purpose-driven life.

Risks of Relying on a Single Income Source

Reliance on a single income source can be risky. If that source is compromised, your financial stability is threatened. Many people experience unexpected job losses, company downsizing, or industries struggling, which can lead to sudden financial instability. Or if you're a freelancer and your main client decides to cut back on spending, you could suddenly lose much of your income. This can lead to financial stress and difficulty paying bills. It also limits your financial growth. With only one source, your income is capped. You can only make as much as that one source allows.

The recent economic changes have shown us how uncertain things can be. Industries that seemed stable have faced unexpected challenges, and many people have found themselves without work overnight. When your financial well-being is tied to one source, any problem with that source becomes a problem for your entire financial health. By having multiple sources of income, you safeguard yourself against the unpredictable nature of employment and market conditions.

Types of Revenue Streams

Understanding the types of income is crucial to building multiple revenue streams. You can develop three types of revenue streams: active, passive, and portfolio income. Each type has its characteristics and can suit different lifestyles and financial goals.

Active Income

Active income is money earned from performing a service or work you actively do. This includes wages, salaries, tips, and money made from businesses with direct involvement. It's the most common form of income because it's how most people are trained to earn money—through a job. It's straightforward but requires your time and effort. Think of a chef cooking in a restaurant. They're actively creating meals and earning money for their time and skill. It's immediate and tangible. With active income, you are trading an hour of your time (your most precious commodity) for a dollar bill (a ubiquitous commodity). This means there's a limit to how much you can earn because there are only so many hours in a day you can work.

Another disadvantage of active income is that many hands are dipping into your hard-earned income. Many laws govern how that money can be earned, accounted for, and paid. Taxes, payments into social security, and other distributions (such as unemployment and health insurance) are usually taken out before you even receive your paycheck. In some cases, such as tips, the money earned may be put into a pool that is then distributed across multiple team members. In the end, active income for most people is extremely limited and does not provide enough for the average family to live on, let alone get out of debt (the GOOD feeling!) and have a fulfilling life.

Passive Income

Passive income is money you earn that requires little to no daily effort to maintain. Some examples include rental income, earnings from a business that does not require direct involvement, earnings from advertisements on a blog or YouTube channel you started, and royalties from books or music you published. The allure of passive income is that it can provide financial security with minimal ongoing work, allowing you more time to focus on other passions or income streams. Once you set up the income stream, it continues to generate money independently.

With passive income, the main point is to do the work one time and get paid for it on an ongoing basis. This means you can earn more income on top of your paycheck with much less effort. Sure, some things like writing a book may take a little time, but you write it once, publish it once, and make money off each sale for as long as the book is listed on a platform such as Amazon or Apple. Now write 5 books, or 20 books, or 50 books, all published and making money continuously without your direct involvement.

You could publish those books in eBook format and sell them on Kindle or audio format and on Audible, creating even more income streams from the same initial single piece of work. This method helps you create a secondary income stream that works while you are busy doing something else. Imagine making money online while you are sleeping—that is the heart of passive income!

Portfolio Income

Portfolio income comes from investments, such as stocks, bonds, and mutual funds. It's money earned from capital gains, dividends, and interest—your money earns more money. For instance, if you buy shares in a company and the value of those shares goes up, you make money if you decide to sell them. It's like planting money seeds and watching them grow.

Real estate, cryptocurrency, and crowdfunding investing also fall under portfolio income. While it might seem like a set-it-and-forget-it type of income, effective portfolio management often requires careful monitoring and adjustment based on market conditions and financial goals. This type of income can fluctuate based on the market, but it can also be a powerful way to grow your wealth over time.

Identifying Personal Goals and Resources

To successfully establish and grow multiple revenue streams, you need first to understand your personal financial goals and the resources you have available. This understanding will help you choose the best income streams to pursue.

Setting Financial Goals

Before you start building multiple revenue streams, it's important to set clear financial goals. Ask yourself: What do I want to achieve with my money? Your financial goals could range from short-term objectives like saving for a vacation to long-term plans like preparing for retirement. Clear goals guide your choices in building income streams. Clear goals also help you stay focused and motivated as you work towards increasing your income through different streams. What do you want your financial garden to look like? A lush oasis of wealth? A steady, reliable source of comfort? Your goals shape your journey.

Celebrate your achievements and progress along the way to stay motivated and maintain momentum.

Setting realistic goals is crucial for success. Unrealistic goals can lead to frustration and burnout. Break down your long-term goals into smaller, manageable steps. When setting goals, it's important to make them **S**pecific, **M**easurable, **A**chievable, **R**elevant, and **T**ime-bound (**SMART**). For example, instead of saying, "I want to save money," you could say, "I want to save $5,000 in the next 12 months for a down payment on a car." This gives you a clear target and a timeframe to work towards and measure your progress.

Assessing Skills and Interests

After setting your goals, assess your skills and interests. What are you good at? What do you enjoy doing? What seeds do you already have to plant? These are potential areas where you could generate income. Understanding these can help you find suitable income streams that match your strengths and passions. Your skills and passions are fertile soil for new income streams.

For instance, if you love graphic design, you might start offering freelance services or selling digital products online. If you're good at writing, you could consider freelancing or starting a blog. If you enjoy photography, you could sell your photos online or offer photography services. You could grow a tech consulting firm if you're a computer whiz. Aligning your income streams with your skills and passions can make the work more enjoyable and sustainable.

Evaluating Available Resources

What tools do you have to cultivate your financial garden? Look at the resources you currently have, such as savings, credit, time, and skills, which can all play a role in developing new income streams. You might invest in stocks or start a small business if you have some savings. Being realistic about what you can commit will help you make better decisions.

Your available time might be limited if you're already working full-time. But, if you have extra time, perhaps you can start a side hustle that aligns with your interests. This is where passive or portfolio income streams can be beneficial because they require less of your time day-to-day. Perhaps you have a network of contacts in a certain industry. You can choose the best income streams for your situation by evaluating your resources. As we close this chapter, consider how different income streams might fit into your life. Remember, the goal isn't just to work harder but to work smarter. By diversifying your income, you protect yourself financially and open new opportunities for growth and freedom.

By the end of this chapter, it's clear that having multiple revenue streams can significantly enhance your financial stability and allow for a more flexible lifestyle. As we move into the next chapter, we'll focus on one of the most dynamic ways to generate multiple income streams: entrepreneurship. We'll explore how starting a small business, developing e-commerce, and freelancing can open new financial opportunities. Let's discover how you can turn your passions into profit by unlocking the potential of entrepreneurship as a powerful revenue stream.

THE ENTREPRENEUR'S JOURNEY

E ntrepreneurship is a thrilling path to earning multiple revenue streams. This chapter dives into what it takes to start a small business, navigate the world of e-commerce, and succeed in freelancing or consulting. Each of these avenues offers unique opportunities and challenges but can significantly contribute to your financial independence and career satisfaction.

Starting a Small Business

Embarking on the journey of starting a small business can be one of the most rewarding ways to create a revenue stream. Whether you're turning a hobby into a full-time job or filling a need in your community, the process involves several key steps that can set the foundation for success. Because starting a small business typically involves providing products or offering services that solve a pain point for customers, this type of entrepreneurship is often called an agency business model.

Identifying Market Needs

The first step in starting a small business is identifying a market need. This involves finding a product or service people want but can't easily get. What products or services are in demand? What gaps exist in the market that you can fill? Conducting market research can help you answer these questions and find a profitable business idea.

You can start by looking at trends and talking to potential customers. What problems do they have? What solutions are they looking for? Are there products or services that are hard to find? To do this, observe the community around you, listen to people's complaints, and think about what could make life easier or better for them.

For example, if your neighborhood lacks a quality bakery and you love baking, this might be an excellent opportunity to open one. Finding a niche market with less competition can be smart, as it allows you to fill a gap and attract customers quickly.

Another avenue to consider is improving a product or service that is provided but has issues. This might involve some research, like talking to potential customers, checking out what competitors are doing, or looking at trends in the industry. Improvements on a product or service can be a great way to build a business if they help solve customers' pain points.

Creating a Business Plan

Once you've identified a market need, the next step is to create a business plan. A business plan is a roadmap for your business. This document outlines your business idea, goals, and methods for achieving these goals. It should include details on what your business will sell, who your customers will be (your customer avatar), how you will produce your product or service, and how much money you expect to make and spend.

A good business plan includes an executive summary, business description, market analysis, organizational structure, product line or services, marketing and sales strategies, funding requirements, and financial projections. A solid business plan is crucial for clarifying your ideas and providing direction and is also necessary if you need to borrow money from a bank or attract investors. They will want to see that you have a thoughtful and feasible plan for success.

The executive summary gives an overview of your business. The business description explains what your company does and what makes it unique. Market analysis involves researching your industry, market size, expected growth, and target market. Organizational structure outlines how your business is set up and who is involved.

The product line or services section describes what you're selling. Marketing and sales strategies explain how you'll attract and retain customers. Funding requirements detail how much money you need to start and run your business. Financial projections show your expected revenue, expenses, and profitability. Creating a business plan helps you stay focused and organized.

Securing Funding and Resources

Most businesses require some form of investment to get off the ground. This could come from savings, bank loans, investments from business partners, friends and family, or even crowdfunding. Evaluating how much money you'll need to start and run your business until it becomes profitable is important. This might include money for equipment, initial product manufacturing, hiring employees, or marketing expenses. Don't forget to account for unexpected expenses.

Personal savings are the most common source of funding for new businesses. You can consider taking out a loan if you don't have enough savings. Various types of loans are available, including small business loans, personal loans, and lines of credit.

Investors are another option, but they typically require giving up some control of your business in exchange for funding. This can include family and friends, angel investors, or venture capitalists. Crowdfunding is a newer option that involves raising small amounts of money from a large number of people. This funding method is an investment income stream for those providing the money, and you can also become involved within your investing income stream strategy.

Starting a small business often requires resources, including the tools, technology, and people you'll need to operate it. Securing the right resources, like finding suppliers or hiring the right team, is crucial for getting your business started on the right footing.

E-commerce and Online Businesses

With the rise of the internet, starting an online business has become a popular and often cost-effective way to enter the world of entrepreneurship. An online business can reach a large audience and isn't limited by geographic location—a boundaryless marketplace.

Setting Up an Online Store

Setting up an online store can be more straightforward and less costly than opening a physical store. You can sell products directly to consumers anywhere in the world to reach a global market. Using e-commerce platforms like Shopify, Etsy, or Amazon makes it relatively easy to start selling online.

To start, you must decide on your product range, set up a website, organize a secure payment processing system, and plan how you will handle shipping. The website should be user-friendly, appealing, and optimized for search engines to attract and retain customers. It's essential to ensure your site is mobile-friendly, as many consumers shop on their phones.

Leveraging Digital Marketing

Once your online store is set up, the next step is attracting customers. Marketing your online store is crucial for attracting customers. Digital marketing is essential for promoting an online business. It involves using social media, email newsletters, paid advertising, and search engine optimization (SEO) to make your business visible to more people. Social media marketing involves using platforms like Facebook, Instagram, TikTok, YouTube, Twitter, and blogs to promote your products and engage with customers. Email marketing involves sending promotional emails to your subscribers. Paid advertising, such as Google Ads, Amazon Ads, and Facebook Ads, can help you reach a larger audience.

Effective digital marketing drives traffic to your website and helps convert visitors into customers. For example, you can use Facebook Ads to target individuals interested in your products or Instagram to showcase your products through beautiful photos and engage with potential customers. Understanding your audience, creating a customer avatar, and how to reach them online is vital to your marketing strategy.

Managing Logistics and Customer Service

Running an online business also means handling logistics, like stocking products and shipping orders. You'll need to figure out how to store your products and the best way to ship them to customers quickly and affordably. Logistics can make or break an online store, so choosing the right shipping partners and having a clear policy is important.

Excellent customer service is also vital, as it helps build customer trust and loyalty. Happy customers are more likely to return and recommend your store, products, or services to others. Respond to customer inquiries quickly and resolve any issues they may have. The main objective is to ensure you create a positive customer shopping experience. Always remember that you are solving your customer's pain points, not creating new ones.

Freelancing and Consulting

For those with specialized skills or knowledge, freelancing or consulting can be a flexible and profitable way to generate income. This path allows you to use your expertise to serve various clients while managing your schedule and projects. Freelancing and consulting can quickly grow into education, coaching, and mentorship. Any form of coaching and education—or knowledge platform—requires the business owner to be knowledgeable and respected within their specific area of expertise. Therefore, this type of entrepreneurship is often called an authoritative business model.

Finding Your Niche

Freelancing and consulting allow you to use your skills to serve various clients rather than working as an employee for a single company. The first step is to find your niche—what are you good at, and what unique value can you offer? Identifying your niche involves finding an area where your skills can solve specific client problems. This could be anything from graphic design, writing, or IT support to more specialized services like legal advice or business/marketing strategy. It also makes it easier to market your services because you can target a specific audience. Remember that YOU are your most valuable product or service, and you are constantly marketing YOU!

Building a Client Base

Once you know your niche, you must start building a client base. Networking, both online and in person, is critical to finding potential clients. Platforms like LinkedIn, freelancing websites like Upwork or Fiverr, industry forums, or even local business events through the MeetUp app can be great places to meet people who might need your services. Referrals from satisfied customers can also be a powerful tool for gaining new business. If you have business clients, ask them to allow you to showcase their name or logo on your website. I want you to know that maintaining a professional online presence and showcasing your previous work, testimonials, or partnerships can greatly enhance credibility.

Managing Projects and Finances

Effective project management keeps clients happy and makes your freelancing or consulting business profitable. This means setting deadlines, communicating regularly with clients, invoicing clients, delivering quality work on schedule, tracking your time, and ensuring you get paid on time. It's also essential to set clear terms and expectations with your clients. This includes agreeing on the scope of work, deadlines, and payment terms. Having clear contracts in place can help prevent misunderstandings and ensure smooth operations. You must also keep records for tax purposes and manage your business expenses carefully to maintain profitability. Using project management and accounting software for invoicing and budget management can help streamline these aspects of the business.

As we wrap up this chapter, we have explored various facets of entrepreneurship and how they can serve as potent revenue streams. Each path offers unique opportunities to grow financially, from small business operations and e-commerce ventures to freelancing skills. This journey requires dedication, research, and resilience but provides a rewarding way to achieve financial independence. Moving into Chapter 3, we will shift our focus to investment income. This next chapter will guide you through the complexities of stock market investments, real estate opportunities, and other investment strategies to further diversify and strengthen your income streams. Let's discover how to make your money work for you through smart investing strategies and how they play a crucial role in your journey toward financial prosperity.

MASTERING THE INVESTMENT LANDSCAPE

I nvestment income is a key component in building and managing multiple revenue streams. This chapter explores different types of investments, including stock market investments, real estate, and alternative investments like peer-to-peer lending and cryptocurrencies. We'll break down the basics, benefits, and strategic approaches to each, helping you make informed decisions that align with your financial goals.

Stock Market Investments

Investing in the stock market is one of the most common ways to build wealth over time. It involves buying shares of companies, and as these companies grow and succeed, so does the value of your investment. These shares can turn into interest, called dividends, or can be sold for a profit, called capital gains.

Basics of Stock Investing

Stock investing starts with understanding the basics of how the stock market works. Investing in the stock market involves buying company shares, representing a small part of the ownership in those companies. When you buy a stock, you become a shareholder and own a part of the company. Typically, these shares give you voting rights for as long as you hold them. Stocks can be bought and sold on stock exchanges, such as the New York Stock Exchange and NASDAQ.

Capital gains and dividends are two main ways to make money from stocks. When the companies do well, the value of their shares typically increases, and you can make money by selling them at a higher price than you paid (capital gains). You might also receive payments made by the company to its shareholders out of its profits (dividends). To start investing in stocks, you need to open a brokerage account, which can be done through traditional brick-and-mortar companies or online platforms that make trading accessible and relatively simple. Researching and choosing stocks wisely is essential, focusing on well-managed, financially stable, and capable growth companies.

Building a Diverse Portfolio

Diversification is key in stock investing. This means spreading your investments across various sectors and types of companies to reduce risk. If one sector or company performs poorly, others in your portfolio may do well, balancing the overall performance. Think of it as **NOT putting all your eggs in one basket. A well-diversified portfolio might include stocks from the technology, healthcare, energy, and consumer goods sectors. Diversification can also occur by** spreading your investments across blue-chip stocks, commodities, or precious metals.

You can also diversify by including different types of stock investments, like mutual funds, which pool money from many investors to buy a broad portfolio of stocks, or exchange-traded funds (ETFs), which are similar but trade like stocks on an exchange. Additionally, investing in bonds, such as municipal bonds, is an excellent avenue for diversification, especially if you are managing for long-term results. When building a portfolio, it's important to consider your risk tolerance, investment goals, and time horizon. This will help you choose the right mix of assets for your situation.

Long-term vs. Short-term Strategies

There are different approaches to stock market investing, mainly long-term and short-term. Long-term investment strategies often involve holding stocks for years, benefiting from the growth of the companies and the overall market. This approach is generally less risky than short-term trading, which involves quickly buying and selling stocks to capitalize on market fluctuations. Short-term trading can be profitable but requires a lot of time, attention, and understanding of market movements, making it riskier and more complex. Long-term investing is safer and less stressful for most people, especially beginners.

Real Estate Investments

Another popular way to generate income is through real estate investing. This involves purchasing property to sell at a higher price or to rent out to tenants. Properties can be acquired through several means.

The typical path to attaining real estate is through a mortgage or other loan type, but you can also acquire real estate through probate or short sale/foreclosure. Another popular and lucrative real estate investment strategy involves purchasing tax liens and deed certificates, which can have a return rate of 5-25% depending on the state and county of acquisition.

Types of Real Estate Investments

Real estate investment can include buying properties to rent out (residential properties), commercial properties (like office buildings and shopping centers), industrial properties (like factories and warehouses), investing in real estate investment trusts (REITs), or even purchasing land. Each type has its own set of benefits and considerations, so choosing the right kind of property to invest in is crucial based on your goals and the amount of time and money you can spend. Owning rental properties can provide regular income through rent payments while paying off the loan (OPM—other people's money). At the same time, REITs offer a way to invest in real estate without buying or managing the property yourself.

Rental Properties and Property Management

One common real estate investment strategy is buying properties to rent out. If you choose to buy property and rent it out, you will gain income from the rent tenants pay. Rental income can be a steady source of cash. However, being a landlord comes with responsibilities like maintaining the property, finding and dealing with tenants, and handling any legal issues that arise. It's important to be prepared for the costs and time involved in property management or consider hiring a property management company to handle these tasks for you, although this will cut into the profits usually by 8-12% of the rent. Hiring a property manager can help you save time and ensure your property is well-maintained.

Real Estate Market Analysis

Successful real estate investing requires understanding the market. This includes knowing about local property values, rent rates, and the economic factors that affect real estate, like future development plans, job growth, and interest rates. Before you purchase, please make sure you research all aspects, including location, history, and property condition. You must also become familiar with local, state, and federal tax and tenant laws. Ensure you do your due diligence in researching everything about the real estate in question. Most research can be done online and through the county clerk's office, sometimes requiring a small fee. Analyzing these factors can help you decide where and when to invest, maximizing your chances of profitability.

Alternative Investments

Besides stocks and real estate, there are other, less traditional ways to invest that can diversify your income streams even further. Loosening restrictions, extending financial borders, and increasing virtual platforms create many different opportunities and innovations for financial investing.

Peer-to-Peer Lending

Peer-to-peer (P2P) lending involves lending money to individuals or businesses through online services that match lenders with borrowers, bypassing traditional banks. Upstart, Prosper, and The Lending Club are popular P2P platforms. As a lender, you can earn interest on the money you lend, which can often be higher than what you would gain from traditional savings and investment routes, usually between 8-18% ROI (return on investment). However, it also carries risks, such as the risk of borrower default. Using reputable platforms and diversifying your lending is important to mitigate these risks.

Cryptocurrencies

Cryptocurrencies like Bitcoin and Ethereum have become popular as an investment class in recent years. They are digital or virtual currencies that use cryptography and blockchain technology for security. These digital currencies operate independently of a central bank and can be bought or sold online. Investing in cryptocurrencies can be highly volatile, meaning the prices can rise or fall drastically in a short period. While they offer high potential returns, the risk is also significant, and it's crucial to research thoroughly and invest cautiously.

Collectibles and Other Non-Traditional Investments

Investing in collectibles such as art, antiques, vintage cars, or rare coins can be another way to diversify your investment portfolio. The value of these items can increase over time, especially if they are rare or become highly sought after. Although these items can appreciate in value over time, their markets can be less predictable and more influenced by trends and personal interests. Collectible investments are more speculative, making them dependent on the market and people's interests. Seek advice from experts. Look for items with a proven track record of increasing in value. This type of investment also requires knowledge about storage and insurance costs. This might be an investment worth considering if you have expertise or a particular interest in a collectible category.

As this chapter on investment income concludes, remember that each type of investment comes with its own risks and rewards. Ask yourself what level of risk you are prepared for. We have seen how various investments can add depth and resilience to your financial portfolio. In Chapter 4, we will shift our focus to passive income streams, such as royalties, affiliate marketing, and digital products. These income sources can provide ongoing revenue with less or minimal active involvement, helping to stabilize and grow your financial foundation as you continue your path to financial independence. Passive income can be crucial in achieving financial independence, allowing you to earn money even when you're not actively working. Get ready to explore how these passive income opportunities can enhance your financial strategy and provide you with more freedom and security.

THE ART OF PASSIVE INCOME

P assive income streams are key to building long-term wealth and financial independence. In this chapter, we'll explore various types of passive income, including royalties and licensing, affiliate marketing, and creating and selling digital products. Once set up, each can provide a steady flow of income with relatively little ongoing effort.

Royalties and Licensing

One of the most creative ways to generate passive income is through royalties and licensing. This involves creating something once, like a book, a song, or software, and then earning money each time someone buys or uses it.

Creating Intellectual Property

Intellectual property (IP) refers to creations of the mind, such as inventions, literary and artistic works, games, designs, trademarks, names, images, and symbols used in commerce. If you create a piece of intellectual property, like a book, music, or a patent, you can earn money through royalties every time someone buys your work or uses your invention. To start earning through royalties, you need to create something unique and then protect it by obtaining copyrights or patents. This protection gives you the exclusive right to use your creation. This can take some time and potentially some legal assistance, but it's a crucial step in ensuring that you are the only one who can authorize the use of your creation.

Licensing Your Work

Licensing involves giving someone else permission to use your IP in exchange for payment. For example, if you invent a new kitchen gadget, you can license the manufacturing rights to a company in return for a fee or a percentage of sales. Another example is a musician might license a song to a company for use in a commercial. In return, the musician receives payments if the commercial is in circulation. Licensing can be a lucrative option because it allows you to profit from your IP without selling it outright or handling the production and distribution yourself. When licensing your work, it's essential to negotiate the terms of the agreement. This includes the licensing fee, how the work can be used, and the length of the license. It's also a good idea to consult a lawyer to protect your rights.

Earning Royalties

Royalties are payments that you receive regularly for allowing others to use your IP. These payments are typically a percentage of the revenue generated by the creation. For instance, if you write a book, you can earn royalties from each sale. Similarly, if you create music, you can earn royalties whenever your music is downloaded, streamed, or played publicly. Setting up royalty income requires some initial effort to create the product and secure a licensing deal. Still, once established, it can provide a steady income stream with little additional work. The amount of royalties you earn depends on the terms of your agreement. It's important to understand how royalties are calculated and when you'll be paid. Royalties provide a continuous income over time, often years after the original work is completed.

Affiliate Marketing

Affiliate marketing is a strategy where you promote other people's products and earn a commission when sales are made through your referral. This can be an effective way to generate income if you have a solid online presence, like a blog, a YouTube channel, or other social media accounts. This is why affiliate marketing is sometimes called network marketing or referral marketing.

Understanding Affiliate Marketing

Affiliate marketing is a type of performance-based marketing in which a business rewards one or more affiliates for each visitor or customer brought by the affiliate's own marketing efforts. As an affiliate, you choose products or services related to your audience's interests and promote them through your website, blog, or social media platforms. You earn a commission each time someone purchases through a link you provide. The link you provide is connected to you through coding embedded in the cookies stored in the internet browser cache. This coding tracks the sale back to your efforts so you can earn a commission. The commission can be a percentage of the sale, a flat rate per sale, or a recurring amount for subscription sales. This setup benefits both the product seller and the marketer—it drives sales for the seller and provides passive income for the marketer.

Choosing the Right Affiliate Programs

Not all affiliate programs are created equal. It's essential to choose ones that offer products or services that are relevant to your audience and are credible and in demand. For example, if you have a blog about fitness, you might join an affiliate program for workout equipment or health supplements. We also suggest you select products or services you use or engage with to aid in testimonials while adding a personal connection to your marketing materials. Look for programs that pay decent commissions, pay on time, and have a good reputation. Also, consider their support, such as marketing materials and training. Many companies have their own affiliate programs, which can be found on their websites, or you can join more extensive networks that connect businesses with affiliate marketers. ClickBank, Shopify, and Amazon are just a few of the affiliate marketing platforms through which you can enter and create your own affiliate marketing business.

Maximizing Affiliate Income

To maximize earnings from affiliate marketing, you need to generate lots of traffic to your promotional links and increase your audience's engagement. The more people you can direct to your affiliate links, the higher your potential earnings. This might involve SEO tactics to rank your blog higher in search engine results, creating valuable content that draws readers, or using social media to reach a broader audience to attract and retain viewers or readers. Share your personal experiences and create tutorials with the product or service. Honest reviews, authentic testimonials, and valuable content can help build trust and encourage more clicks and purchases.

Using multiple channels to promote your affiliate links can also help increase your income. This can include your blog, social media, and email newsletters. Experiment with different strategies to see what works best for your audience. The more people who visit and click on your links, the more potential sales and, therefore, the more commission you can earn.

Creating and Selling Digital Products

Digital products like ebooks, courses, artwork, or software can be a great source of passive income. Once created, these products can be sold repeatedly and on multiple platforms without needing inventory or shipping. Certain digital products, such as ebooks and online courses, can create a passive income stream without you even having to be actively involved in the entire sales process—just make money while you're sleeping.

Types of Digital Products

There are many types of digital products you can create. If you have expertise in a subject, write an ebook or make an online course. If you're artistic, digital artwork or design templates could be your product. Software tools and apps are other popular digital products that cater to specific needs or solve everyday problems. Digital products are items that can be sold and delivered online. The beauty of digital products is that you only have to create them once, and you can sell

them unlimited times without additional costs. The key is to create
something valuable that people are willing to pay for.

Platforms for Selling

There are many platforms where you can sell your digital products.
Selling your digital products can be done through your website or various online marketplaces specializing in digital goods. They also make
it relatively easy to reach large audiences. Websites like Etsy, Amazon,
or your site can be effective. Tools like Shopify or WooCommerce
make setting up an online store easy. For digital courses, platforms like
Udemy or Teachable provide the structure and customer base to help
you succeed.

Each platform has its own set of rules and fees, so choosing the right
one for your product type and audience is important. Consider factors
like fees, ease of use, and the ability to reach your target audience.
Using specific online platforms that handle printing and shipping,
their secure payment processing systems, and an email system, you can
create a fully automated system that operates while you are sleeping,
relaxing at the beach, or spending time with your family.

Marketing Digital Products

Effective marketing is critical to successful digital product sales. Without effective marketing, it's hard for people to find and buy your
products. Start by creating a website or landing page to showcase your
products. Use SEO techniques to attract organic traffic and make it
easy for people to find you online.

This can involve email marketing, content marketing, social media campaigns, your website, and paid advertising to promote your

products or services. Offering free samples or a free chapter can help attract buyers by giving them a taste of what they can expect. You can provide a lead magnet, such as a short ebook in a welcome email, that can be a way to attract customers by offering something of value and showing your authoritative position on the specific subject. Collecting customer emails for future product announcements can also help maintain ongoing sales. Innovation and creativity are essential in marketing campaigns of all kinds.

As we move forward, we've covered how passive income streams like royalties, affiliate marketing, and digital products can bolster your financial stability with continuous income. These income sources require some upfront work and maintenance but can provide earnings for years to come. In Chapter 5, we'll delve into strategies for managing and scaling these revenue streams more effectively. We'll discuss time management, financial tracking, and methods to scale and grow your income sources without becoming overwhelmed. This will equip you with the knowledge to not only sustain but also expand your financial portfolio efficiently. Get ready to learn how to streamline and enhance your multiple revenue streams as we continue our journey toward achieving financial prosperity.

MAXIMIZING YOUR FINANCIAL POTENTIAL

A s you diversify and grow your income through multiple revenue streams, managing them effectively becomes crucial. This
chapter focuses on time management and productivity, financial
management and tracking, and scaling and growing your income
streams. By mastering these areas, you can sustain and multiply your
efforts, leading to tremendous financial success and stability.

Time Management and Productivity

Efficient time management is crucial when you are juggling multiple
revenue streams. It ensures that you can focus on each income source
without feeling overwhelmed or burnt out.

Prioritizing Tasks

Effective time management starts with prioritizing your tasks based on their importance and urgency. Start each day or week by listing what you need to do for each income stream and then rank these tasks. Use tools like calendars, to-do lists, and project management software to track what needs to be done and when. This helps ensure you spend the right amount of time on each task and pay attention to your income sources.

For multiple revenue streams, determine which tasks are critical for maintaining income and which are aimed at growth. This will help you focus on activities that offer the greatest returns—income-generating activities are the most significant activities you need to focus on. Suppose you have activities that are not centered on generating income. In that case, you should delegate them to other team members, hire individuals to complete them, or find ways to eliminate them.

Efficient Time Allocation

Allocating your time efficiently involves dividing your day into blocks dedicated to different tasks. This technique, known as time blocking, can help you focus on one income stream at a time, reducing the stress of multitasking, improving productivity, and eliminating mistakes. For instance, you might dedicate mornings to managing your online store, afternoons to consulting clients, and evenings to researching new investment opportunities. For example, if you have three income streams, you might dedicate mornings to one, afternoons to another, and evenings to the third, or alternate days for each. Staying focused on one income stream at a time avoids multitasking, which can seriously reduce your productivity and profitability. Online apps such as Google Calendar or Trello can help you create, prioritize, and schedule tasks and time blocking.

Avoiding Burnout

It's easy to feel overwhelmed when managing multiple revenue streams. Burnout can happen when you're overworked and stressed, leading to exhaustion and decreased productivity. To avoid burnout, it's important to schedule regular breaks and downtime. Make sure to balance work with leisure activities that you enjoy. Maintaining a healthy lifestyle, including regular exercise, healthy eating, and adequate sleep, can help you stay energized and focused. Set realistic goals, and don't overcommit. Doing a few things well is better than spreading yourself too thin. Make time for hobbies, exercise, and spending time with family and friends. Keeping your work-life balance in check is essential for long-term success and health.

Financial Management and Tracking

Proper financial management is another pillar of maintaining multiple revenue streams. Monitoring where money is coming from and going helps you make informed decisions about your financial strategies.

Budgeting and Expense Tracking

Keeping a close eye on your finances is essential when you have multiple income streams. Use budgeting tools or software to track your income and expenses from each source. This will help you understand which streams are the most profitable, where you may need to cut costs, or which may need restructuring or elimination. Budgeting apps like QuickBooks or NerdWallet and spreadsheets keep everything organized and accessible. List all your income sources and fixed expenses, like rent or mortgage payments, utilities, and groceries. Track your variable expenses as well to see where your money is going. This helps you identify areas where you can cut costs and save more money. Using these tools can also aid you in identifying those revenue-generating activities on which you need to spend the most time.

Tax Considerations

Managing taxes can be complex with multiple income streams, especially if they span different types of income, such as salary, freelance payments, and investment returns. For example, income from a job is usually subject to income tax, while investment income might be subject to capital gains tax. It is wise to consult a tax professional to help you take advantage of deductions and credits and ensure compliance with tax laws. Keeping detailed records of all your financial transactions is crucial for accurate tax reporting. This includes asking for and keeping all business-related receipts. Keep all your physical records for each income stream together and separate from other income streams and your personal records.

Financial Planning and Forecasting

Financial planning involves setting short-term and long-term financial goals and developing strategies to reach them. This might include retirement savings, paying off debt, or building an emergency fund. Use past performance and forecasting to predict future income and expenses based on current trends in your various income streams. Your market research should also include new technologies or emerging trends with which you may have to become involved. This planning helps you anticipate changes and adjust your strategies. Forecasting can help you make informed decisions about where to invest more time and money and where to cut back. Regularly review your financial goals and progress, adjusting your plans as necessary to stay on track.

Scaling and Growing Income Streams

Once you have established multiple revenue streams, the next step is to scale and grow these sources to increase your income.

Reinvesting Profits

One of the best ways to grow your income streams is to reinvest your profits. For example, profits from a rental property could be used to renovate the property, allowing you to increase rent. You could use earnings from your freelance work to fund marketing or product development for your online store. Another example is investing your stock dividends into purchasing more shares. Reinvesting helps compound earnings and can accelerate the growth of revenue streams. The key is to use your profits to create more income opportunities.

Automating and Outsourcing

As your income streams grow, consider automating tasks or outsourcing them to freelancers or virtual assistants (VA). This can free up your time to focus on high-value (income-generating) activities that can expand your businesses, such as strategizing, networking, and creating new products or services. Identify repetitive tasks that can be automated with software, such as invoicing or email marketing.

Zapier, HubSpot, and Airtable are popular apps for automating tasks. Automation tools can also be used to schedule social media posts, send email newsletters, and manage finances.

Outsourcing involves hiring others to handle tasks you don't have time for or aren't skilled at. Consider outsourcing tasks not central to your business but necessary, such as accounting, SEO, or customer service. This might include hiring a virtual assistant to handle administrative tasks, a marketer to manage your advertising, or a developer to build your website. The emergence of AI (artificial intelligence) bots and agents has vastly improved customer service, email campaigns, appointment makers, and reminders while making such services more cost-effective. Popular AI bot and agent platforms for emails and customer service include Intercom, ADA, and LivePerson.

Expanding into New Markets

You can look for opportunities to expand your successful income streams into new markets. This might involve targeting a different demographic, expanding internationally, or offering new products or services that complement what you already offer. Market research is crucial to understanding the needs and preferences of new potential customers and emerging technologies and trends. For example, if you have a successful online store, consider expanding into international markets. This might involve translating your website, adjusting your marketing strategy, and navigating different regulations and shipping requirements. Expanding into new markets can help you reach more customers and increase your income.

Building a Strong Network

Your network is your net worth—your connections and relationships with other people directly impact your overall financial and business success (Porter Gale). Networking is an important part of building and managing multiple revenue streams. Building a solid network can provide valuable opportunities, support, and resources. Attend industry events, join professional organizations, and participate in online communities to connect with others in your field. Networking can help you find new clients, partners, and opportunities for collaboration. It can also provide support and advice from others with experience managing multiple revenue streams.

Continuing Education and Skill Development

The world is constantly changing, and staying up to date with new trends, technologies, and best practices can help you stay competitive. Continuing education and skill development are crucial for long-term success. Take advantage of online courses, workshops, and seminars to continue learning and developing your skills. This can help you improve your income streams and identify new growth opportunities.

Monitoring and Adjusting Your Strategy

Track your progress and evaluate your performance regularly. Use tools like spreadsheets, dashboards, and reports to monitor your income, expenses, and other vital metrics. Identify areas where you're doing well and where you can improve through key performance indicators (KPIs). Adjust your strategy as needed to achieve your goals and stay on track.

Learning from Failure

Failure and setbacks are a natural part of the process. Learning from failure can help you grow and improve. When things don't go as planned, analyze what went wrong and why. Use this information to make better decisions and avoid similar mistakes in the future. Failure can be a valuable learning experience that helps you build resilience and improve your strategies.

Seeking Support and Advice

Seeking support and advice from others can help you succeed. Don't be afraid to ask for help when you need it. Reach out to mentors, advisors, and peers for support and guidance. Join professional organizations and online communities to connect with others who have experience managing multiple revenue streams. Sharing experiences and advice can provide valuable insights and help you overcome challenges.

As we wrap up this chapter on managing and growing your multiple revenue streams, remember that the journey to financial independence requires continuous learning and adaptation. By effectively managing your time, finances, and growth strategies, you can enhance the stability and profitability of your various income sources. In the concluding chapter of this book, we will recap the key points discussed throughout and offer some final thoughts on your journey toward achieving financial prosperity. Let's reflect on what we've learned and consider how to apply these insights to achieve your financial goals.

FROM VISION TO VICTORY

Throughout this book, we have explored the significance of building multiple revenue streams and how they can contribute to achieving financial independence. We've covered a wide range of topics, from the basics of earning from various sources to the details of managing and expanding those income streams. The journey toward diversified income is both exciting and essential in today's economic landscape, where relying on a single source of income is increasingly risky.

Recap of Key Points

As we review each of the chapters and their key points, ask yourself: how does this step fit into my financial plan? How can I turn this into a potential income stream? What expertise, abilities, or skillsets can I use to build this income stream? Please write out your answers and think constructively about each key point. Some parts of this book may not apply to you individually, but we are confident there are some areas you can implement into your life somehow, somewhere and some way to aid you in your financial situation.

The Importance of Financial Diversification

We began by understanding the critical need for financial diversification. We saw how relying on a single income source can be risky and limiting. Just like a gardener plants various types of seeds to ensure at least some will grow, diversifying your income ensures that if one stream dries up or has troubles, others can sustain your financial needs. This approach minimizes risk and provides a safety net for unexpected economic changes but can also open opportunities for greater financial freedom and independence.

Multiple Revenue Streams

In the first chapter, we explored the different types of revenue streams: active, passive, and portfolio income. Each type offers unique advantages and can be tailored to fit different lifestyles and financial goals. Understanding and implementing multiple revenue streams can help you build a more secure and robust financial future.

Entrepreneurship and Business

Chapter two focused on entrepreneurship as a vital source of revenue. Starting a small business, venturing into e-commerce, and freelancing are all ways to create new income opportunities. Each option requires different strategies and approaches, from identifying market needs to leveraging digital marketing and managing customer relations.

Investment Income

In the third chapter, we discussed investment as a significant component of income diversification. From the stock market to real estate and alternative investments like peer-to-peer lending and cryptocurrencies, we covered how to start, what to consider, and ways to minimize risks while maximizing returns.

Passive Income Streams

Chapter four delved into passive income streams such as royalties, affiliate marketing, and selling digital products. Passive income streams are especially valuable because they can generate money continuously with minimal ongoing effort after the initial setup. This aspect of financial diversification is attractive because it allows you to earn while focusing on other pursuits or even while you sleep.

Managing and Growing Your Income

Finally, Chapter Five covered strategies for effectively managing and growing your income streams. From budgeting and tax considerations to automating and expanding into new markets, these strategies help you maintain and amplify your financial gains.

Encouragement for Continued Learning and Growth

The path to financial prosperity is ongoing, and the landscape of income opportunities constantly evolves and requires constant learning and adaptation. Economic conditions change, new technologies emerge, and personal goals evolve. It's crucial to stay informed and adaptable. Continue learning about new ways to manage and diversify your income. Attend workshops, read books, and perhaps most importantly, engage with communities of entrepreneurs and investors who are also on this journey. Learning from peers and mentors can help you avoid common pitfalls while providing insights and opportunities you might not find alone.

Final Thoughts on Achieving Financial Prosperity

Achieving financial prosperity through multiple revenue streams is a realistic goal for anyone willing to put in the effort to understand and manage their finances intelligently. It's about more than just making money—it's about making wise financial decisions to provide security and wealth for the future. It requires diligence, creativity, and a willingness to learn and adapt. Financial prosperity is a willingness to step out of your comfort zone and take calculated risks. Remember, financial diversification aims to increase your income and build a stable, secure financial foundation to live your desired life. Whether that means having more time to spend with family, the ability to travel, or the freedom to retire early, financial independence gives you choices.

Call to Action

As you finish this book, don't let your journey stop here. Now is the time to take the first step if you haven't already or to push further if you're already on your way. Review the strategies discussed in this book and identify one or two that you haven't tried yet. Maybe that means sketching out a business idea, researching investments, or setting up a meeting with a financial advisor. Whatever your next step is, commit to taking it. Make a plan for how you will implement them in the coming months. Set small, specific, achievable goals and steadily work towards them. Celebrate your successes along the way and learn from any setbacks.

Remember, the journey to diversified income and financial independence takes time. It's made up of small, consistent actions taken daily. Every step you take is a step towards greater financial security and freedom. Remember, baby steps—progress, not perfection. Repetition and practice do not make perfect; they only make permanence. Keep pushing forward, keep learning, and keep diversifying. Your financial future is in your hands—shape it with intention and confidence!

MAKE A DIFFERENCE WITH YOUR REVIEW

D ear Reader,

    Thank you for exploring the financial strategies detailed in **"Pathways to Prosperity: Unlocking Multiple Revenue Streams to Financial Independence**." We hope the insights and guidance provided in this book empower you to build a robust and diversified financial portfolio, paving your way toward financial independence.

Your words have power. They can inspire, enlighten, and transform. By sharing your experience with **"Pathways to Prosperity**," you're not just leaving a review - you're lighting the way for others on their financial journey.

Think about the last time a book changed your life. Remember that feeling of excitement, of possibilities opening up before you. Your review can give that same gift to someone else. You join a community of dreamers and doers when you share your thoughts. People just like you are seeking financial freedom and a life of abundance. Your voice matters in this conversation.

Imagine someone standing at a crossroads, unsure which path to take. Your review could be the sign they need, pointing them toward financial independence and a brighter future. You're planting seeds of change by taking a few moments to write your review. Those seeds will grow, spreading knowledge and hope to others hungry for financial wisdom.

Your generosity in sharing your experience ripples out into the world. It touches lives you may never meet but whose futures you help shape. Are you ready to make a difference? To be a beacon for others on their financial journey? Your review is the first step. Let's create a wave of positive change, starting right now.

Why Your Reviews Matter

Your reviews make a world of difference in helping us reach more readers:

- **Feedback to the Author**: Your insights provide valuable feedback that influences future publications and helps us better serve you.

- **Helps Other Readers**: Reviews help increase the visibility of our books, making it easier for other readers to discover and access valuable resources.

- **Community Impact**: By sharing your experience, you contribute to a community of like-minded individuals working towards better financial health and independence.

- **Support Quality Content**: By sharing your review, you contribute to the quality and success of publications that aim to educate and inspire.

- **Improve Future Editions**: Constructive feedback helps us enhance the content and structure of future editions.

How to Write a Helpful Review

No matter where you leave your review, we sincerely appreciate your time and effort in providing valuable insights. Here are some tips on review writing:

- **Be Specific**: Please make sure to mention what you liked about the book and how it impacted your financial management approach.

- **Be Honest**: Feel free to share any criticisms or areas where the book could be improved. Honest feedback is invaluable.

- **Include Details**: Discuss particular noteworthy chapters or concepts and explain why.

Connect With Us

We would love to hear more about your journey and how "Pathways to Prosperity" has influenced your approach to financial diversification. Connect with us on social media to stay updated on upcoming books, events, and helpful tips:

- Facebook: https://www.facebook.com/profile.php?id=61556836797998

- Website: https://schulzpublishing.com/

Again, thank you for your support and being a part of the Schulz Publishing community. We look forward to reading your reviews and hearing about your success stories!

Best regards,

Schulz Publishing

REFERENCES

Agarwal, M. (2024, January 18). *10 passive income ideas to secure your financial future and create wealth*. BlueHost.com. https://www.bluehost.com/blog/passive-income-ideas/?utm_ca mpaign=pmax_PPC&utm_source=googleads&utm_medium=ge nericsearch&channelid=P61C101S570N0B5578A2D4499E0000 V338&ds_k=&gad_source=1&gclid=Cj0KCQjw1qO0BhDwA RIsANfnkv_pejX3N4AwUokfRVnjLwjWJItkw8RteXJ_TXm4 UoUB_CxNA8PmVS8aApT_EALw_wcB&gclsrc=aw.ds

Allen, R. G. (2002). *Multiple streams of income: How to generate a lifetime of unlimited wealth*. Wiley.

Anthropic. (2023). Claude [Large language model]. Retrieved from https://www.anthropic.com

Bard. (2024). Gemini [Computer-generated text]. Retrieved from h ttps://gemini.google.com/

Bavaria, S. (2020). *The income factory: An investor's guide to consistent lifetime returns*. McGraw Hill.

Chen, J. (2024, April 16). *Investing: An introduction*. Investopedia. com. https://www.investopedia.com/articles/basics/11/3-s-simp le-investing.asp

Corporate Finance Institute (CFI). (n.d.). *Passive income*. Corporat eFinanceInstitute.com. https://corporatefinanceinstitute.com/re sources/accounting/passive-income/

Coursera. (2024, April 3). *Affiliate marketing: What it is and how to get started*. Coursera.com. https://www.coursera.org/articles/affi liate-marketing

DeVuyst, S. (2022, July 19). *5 things I've learned about building passive income*. Honeybook.com. https://www.honeybook.com/blog/5-things-ive-learned-about-b uilding-passive-income?utm_source=google&utm_campaign=18 541494861&utm_medium=cpc&utm_content=&utm_term=& placement=143815977802&device=c&gclsrc=aw.ds&gad_source =1&gclid=Cj0KCQjw1qO0BhDwARIsANfnkv_2GVR8TabXq ArZ-vXvK6AWG-9D6jcGefacya7_HDcvFT10hJ7uPwQaAoNB EALw_wcB

Dove, G. (2024, June 19). *The transformative power of the knowl-edge business model: How it changes people and society*. LinkedIn. com. https://www.linkedin.com/pulse/transformative-power-kn owledge-business-model-how-changes-gloria-dove-omszf/

Elorus. (2024, March 7). *Agency business model: How to choose the right one for your digital agency*. Elorus.com. https://www.elorus.com /blog/agency-business-model/

Fidelity. (2023, September 20). *Why diversification matters*. Fideli ty.com. https://www.fidelity.com/learning-center/investment-pr oducts/mutual-funds/diversification

Flynn, P. (n.d.). *Affiliate marketing: A simple step by step guide*. Sma rtPassiveIncome.com. https://www.smartpassiveincome.com/gu ides/affiliate-marketing-strategies/

Fox, S. (2012). *Click millionaires: Work less, live more with an internet business you love*. American Management Association.

Gabrielle, G. (2019). *Passive income freedom: 23 passive income blue-prints*. SassyZenGirl.com.

Gale, P. (2013). *Your network is your net worth: Unlock the hidden power of connections for wealth, success, and happiness in the digital age*. Atria Books.

Houston, M. (2024, February 2). *Why adding passive income streams to your business is a good idea*. Forbes.com. https://www.forbes.com/sites/melissahouston/2024/02/02/why -adding-passive-income-streams-to-your-business-is-a-good-idea/

Investopedia. (2024, February 1). *Affiliate marketer: Definition, ex-amples, and how to get started*. Investopedia.com. https://www.in-vestopedia.com/terms/a/affiliate-marketing.asp

Kiyosaki, R. T. (2017). *Rich dad poor dad* (2nd ed.). Plata Publishing.

Koe, D. (2023, April 14). *The micro education business model: How to monetize your knowledge*. TheDanKoe.com . https://thedankoe.com/letters/the-new-wave-of-micro-busines ses-monetize-your-knowledge/

Koumadoraki, A. (2022, November 21). *7 revenue-generat-ing business models in the knowledge economy*. LearnWorlds .com. https://www.learnworlds.com/knowledge-economy-busi-ness-models/

Leavitt, K. (2023, December 19). *Why every entrepreneur should consider launching a knowledge business*. Keap.com. https://keap.com/small-business-automation-blog/growth/perso

nal-development/why-every-entrepreneur-should-consider-launc
hing-a-knowledge-business

Lioudis, N. (2022, June 15). *The importance of diversification*. Inve
stopedia.com. https://www.investopedia.com/investing/importa
nce-diversification/

Mailchimp. (n.d.). *7 types of business models to consider for your
company*. MailChimp.com.
https://mailchimp.com/resources/types-of-business-models/?ds_
c=DEPT_AOC_Google_Search_US_EN_NB_Acquire_Broad_
DSA-Rsrc_US&ds_kids=p78250621731&ds_a_lid=dsa-222702
6702184&ds_cid=71700000115207178&ds_agid=58700008574
686663&gad_source=1&gclid=Cj0KCQjw1qO0BhDwARIsAN
fnkv82l08DcI1QqHH6420K-QgLTSNRGmdo7Rjm38px83Ik6
vXvsWjkrQkaAopREALw_wcB&gclsrc=aw.ds

Malnik, J. (2023, June 20). *Most profitable business models for agencies:
According to 20 agencies*. Databox.com. https://databox.com/age
ncy-business-models-profitability

Marsh McLennan Agency. (2023, December 21). *The importance of
diversifying investments in the face of economic uncertainty*. Mars
hMMA.com. https://www.marshmma.com/us/insights/details/
the-importance-of-diversifying-investments.html

Nightingale-Conant. (2019). *The power of passive income: Make your
money work for you*. Entrepreneur Press.

Ong, S. Q. (2023, May 25). *Affiliate marketing for beginners: What it
is and how to succeed*. AHRefs.com. https://ahrefs.com/blog/affil
iate-marketing/

OpenAI. (2024). ChatGPT [Large language model]. Retrieved from
https://chat.openai.com/

Patel, N. (n.d.). *The complete guide to affiliate marketing*. NeilPatel.
com. https://neilpatel.com/what-is-affiliate-marketing/

Patterson, M. (2021, October 11). *The agency business model: Is it right for you?* BSFreeBusiness.com. https://bsfreebusiness.com/the-agency-business-model-is-it-right-for-you/

Riley, R. (2024). *The 50 best passive income streams anybody can master: Learn how to make money online quickly, create wealth, and achieve financial freedom*. Rick Riley.

Royal, J. (2023, June 16). *Why is portfolio diversification important for investors?* Bankrate.com. https://www.bankrate.com/investing/diversification-is-important-in-investing/

Schulz, M. R. (2024). *Creating daily habits: A simple guide to building healthy routines that achieve your goals, build life skills, and improve productivity*. Schulz Publishing.

Schulz, M. R. (2024). *Unlock the entrepreneurial dream by starting your LLC: Your stress-free journey to swiftly establish, legally protect, and strategically expand your small business by paving the way to prosperity*. Schulz Publishing.

Shopify. (2024, May 6). *What is affiliate marketing? Everything you need to know in 2024; Here's how you can break into an $8 billion industry full of opportunities to make passive income*. Shopify.com. https://www.shopify.com/blog/affiliate-marketing

Stanley, T. J., & Danko, W. D. (2016). *The millionaire next door: The surprising secrets of America's wealthy* (20th ed.). Taylor Trade Publishing.

U.S. Securities and Exchange Commission. (n.d.). *Introduction to investing*. Investor.gov. https://www.investor.gov/introduction-investing

Waddington, S. (2015, September 5). *How to run an agency. Five business models*. LinkedIn.com. https://www.linkedin.com/pulse/how-run-agency-five-business-models-stephen-waddington/

Yochim, D. (2023, May 17). *Investing 101: A guide to investing basics*. NerdWallet.com. https://www.nerdwallet.com/article/investing/investing-101

Yoshida, H. (2022, September 23). *Understanding the importance of investment diversification*. Forbes.com. https://www.forbes.com/sites/forbesfinancecouncil/2022/09/23/understanding-the-importance-of-investment-diversification/

www.ingramcontent.com/pod-product-compliance
Lightning Source LLC
Chambersburg PA
CBHW072051040426
42447CB00012BB/3092